LIGHTHOUSES OF CALIFORNIA

Help Us Keep This Guide Up to Date

Every effort has been made by the authors and editors to make this guide as accurate and useful as possible. However, many things can change after a guide is published—phone numbers change, facilities come under new management, etc.

We would love to hear from you concerning your experiences with this guide and how you feel it could be improved and be kept up to date. While we may not be able to respond to all comments and suggestions, we'll take them to heart and we'll also make certain to share them with the authors. Please send your comments and suggestions to the following address:

> The Globe Pequot Press
> Reader Response/Editorial Department
> P. O. Box 480
> Guilford, CT 06437

Or you may e-mail us at:

> editorial@GlobePequot.com

Thanks for your input, and happy travels!

LIGHTHOUSES SERIES

LIGHTHOUSES OF CALIFORNIA
A Guidebook and Keepsake

Bruce Roberts and Ray Jones

INSIDERS' GUIDE®

GUILFORD, CONNECTICUT
AN IMPRINT OF THE GLOBE PEQUOT PRESS

INSIDERS' GUIDE®

Text design by Schwartzman Design, Deep River, CT
Map design and terrain by Stephen C. Stringall, Cartography by M.A. Dubé
Map ©The Globe Pequot Press
All photographs, unless otherwise credited, are by Bruce Roberts.

Library of Congress Cataloging-in-Publication Data
Roberts, Bruce, 1930-
   Lighthouses of California : a guidebook and keepsake / Bruce Roberts and Ray Jones.
—1st ed.
       p. cm. — (Lighthouses series)
   ISBN 0-7627-3735-2
       1. Lighthouses—California—Guidebooks. I. Jones, Ray, 1948- II. Title. III. Lighthouses series (Globe Pequot Press)

VK1024.C2R63 2005
387.1'55'09794—dc22
                                                        2004060824

Manufactured in China
First Edition/First Printing

The information listed in this guide was confirmed at press time. The ownership of many lighthouses, however, is gradually being transferred from the Coast Guard to private concerns. Please confirm visitor information before traveling.

CONTENTS

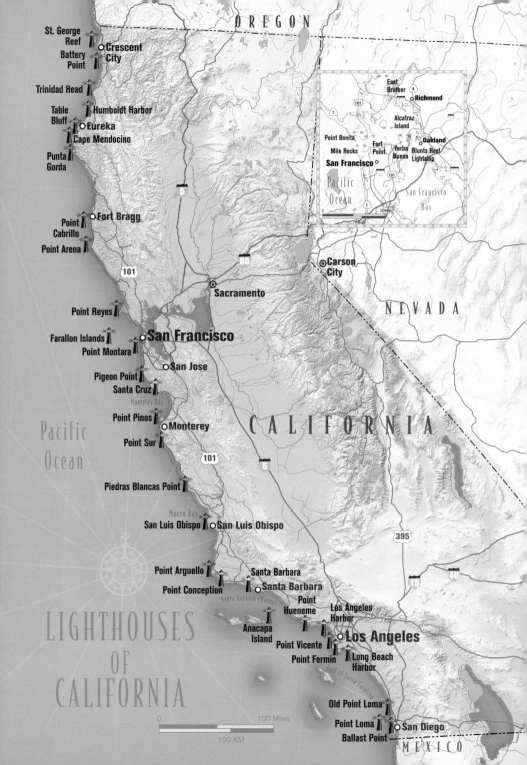

INTRODUCTION

California is where America reaches its limit, for here the continent comes to an abrupt and spectacular end. Here the "westward-ho" migrations of the pioneers were finally halted. They could go no farther, for California lies at the edge of an ocean more than 5,000 miles wide. So vast is the Pacific that it is larger by far than all the earth's landmasses combined.

The Pacific is so enormous and so stormy that throughout human history only the bravest mariners have challenged it. We will never know how many paid for their daring with their lives, but the number, if we knew it, would be impressive. No doubt, many simply vanished into the ocean's trackless, watery wastes. Many others came to grief at the margins of the Pacific, near where, at long last, it touches land. California is one such place, and from the point of view of mariners, far more threatening than most.

Along the 840 miles of the California coastline, the transition from land to water is abrupt. In many places lofty desert mountains drop straight down into the waves, and offshore, lesser peaks rise from the ocean floor to lurk just beneath the surface. The prevailing westerly winds are likely to drive vessels much closer to shore than their captains intend, often times with deadly results. So dangerous is the California coast that, unless they are headed for port, wise navigators plot a course many miles from the nearest landfall.

To help ships keep a respectful distance or find safe harbor, in the 1850s the U.S. government established a string of powerful navigational lights reaching from San Diego to Crescent City. These are the California coastal lighthouses, and together with a few scattered harbor lights, they are the subject of this book. Much of the information you'll find in *Lighthouses of California* is historical in nature, for most of these lonely sentinels have stood for more than a century. The first were built only a few years after the gold rush began to attract huge fleets and hordes of immigrants to California.

Before that time, however, the California coast was dark and largely uncharted. Indeed, for centuries California was so poorly understood that many mapmakers and mariners, believed it was an island. Although he had never seen it, the early sixteenth-century Spanish novelist Montalvo described California as an island inhabited entirely by warrior women "robust of body, strong and passionate in heart, and of great valor. Their island is one of the most rugged in the world with bold rocks and crags. Their arms are

A carriage of iron and brass supports the Point Reyes Light.

all of gold as are the harnesses of the wild beasts, which after taming, they ride. In all the island there is no other metal." Sailing northward from western Mexico, early Spanish explorers kept testing the "island" claim by trying to sail completely around California or, at least, take on board a few Amazons or a little gold. Most turned back or perished long before they learned the truth.

Likely, the adventurer Juan Rodriguez Cabrillo knew better than to accept Montalvo's claim at face value when he sailed from Navidad in western Mexico (New Spain) in June 1542, just half a century after Columbus arrived in America. With two small ships, the *Victoria* and *Salvador*, and a crew of about 250, Cabrillo pushed slowly northward, reaching San Diego Bay in late September. Cabrillo and his men then made their way up the coast as far north as present-day Oregon before finally turning around for home—a destination the explorer would never reach. Cabrillo died from injuries from a fall he took on shore, probably somewhere near Point Reyes. Cabrillo's expedition succeeded in bringing the first Europeans to California and proving beyond reasonable doubt that it was not an island and not inhabited by a mysterious race of Amazons, without the aid of charts or navigational lights.

Long before the United States had a presence in California, the Spanish lit fires on Point Loma and elsewhere along the coast to call their ships in from the sea. To mark channels and guide supply vessels to the mission and presidio at San Diego, bright candles were hung from poles; otherwise, the king's mariners were forced to navigate the dangerous coast without the help of lights on the shore. Then came Mexican independence, the Mexican general Santa Anna, and the Mexican war with the United States. By the time the Treaty of Guadalupe Hidalgo ceded California to the United States in 1848, the old Spanish lights had gone dark.

The ink on the treaty was hardly dry before the discovery of gold in the Sierra foothills turned California into a passion for Americans. Suddenly, the Far West was seen as more than a place where formerly landless easterners carved out hardscrabble home-steads. It had a value that could be counted out in dollars—a lot of them. It offered not only cheap land and plenty of it but also the opportunity to get rich quick. The California gold rush was on.

Thousands of miles of wilderness separated the settled eastern states from the nation's newest and apparently richest seaboard. Most of the would-be millionaires who wanted to go to California and pan for gold would have to get there by ship. The nation could never hope to settle and exploit the West without a secure coastline, inviting to maritime commerce.

Graveyard of the Pacific

It took hundreds of years for colonists to populate North America's East Coast. Even at this relatively leisurely pace, the settlement of the East had exacted a heavy toll. Thousands of ships were broken up by hurricanes, driven onto beaches and shattered by gales, or smashed by uncharted sandbars; uncounted thousands of sailors and passengers were drowned. The West was likely to be built up much faster than the East had been, and it was even less friendly to ships and sailors. Its shoreline stretched more than 2,000 rock-strewn miles, from Cape Flattery in the north to San Diego in the south. Most maritime disasters happen not on the open sea but near the coast. For as long as ships have sailed the seas, sailors have paid with their lives when their vessels have come too close to the shore. Ships are built to withstand the stresses of high winds and giant waves, but a collision with rock, reef, or sand is usually fatal.

Unfortunately for many, such deadly encounters between ship and shore are common along the American West Coast. Stony capes jut out into the ocean like knife blades. Massive blocks of stone rise up unexpectedly from the waves. Swift-running streams wash mud and gravel out of the mountains to form ship-killing shallows and block off the entrances of the rivers, where sea captains might otherwise find safe harbor from a storm.

In the East, Cape Hatteras has won the dubious distinction of "the graveyard of the Atlantic." But the West has no one maritime hazard that stands out from the others. All of the West Coast is a graveyard for ships and sailors, especially the California coast.

Lighting the West

To help mariners navigate safely in the face of these dangers, the U.S. Congress launched an ambitious construction program in the 1850s aimed at raising lighthouse towers at strategic locations along the West Coast. Generally speaking, lighthouses perform two key services: They help pilots and navigators keep their ships on course, and they warn of impending calamity. The latter is, of course, their most vital and dramatic function. Lighthouses save ships and lives.

Government lighthouse officials hurried a survey team to the West in 1848. Its members painstakingly navigated the wild and dangerous western shores. On more than one occasion the survey ships themselves came near disaster for lack of adequate charts and shore lights to guide their pilots. But the surveyors persevered, approaching treacherous headlands, sizing up dangerous rocks, charting capes and points, noting likely construction sites, even meeting with local Indian chiefs to see if their tribes were hostile and likely to attack construction crews.

The team compiled a report recommending establishment of a string of lighthouses from Canada to Mexico. The report pointed to locations where the need for coastal markers was most critical—key harbors, important river entrances, threatening rocks and reefs. By 1852 Congress had narrowed the survey list to sixteen sites where construction of lighthouses was to begin immediately. Among those with congressional authorization were Alcatraz Island, Fort Point, Point Bonita, and the Farallon Islands near San Francisco; Point Loma, Santa Barbara, Point Pinos, and Point Conception along the southern California coast; and Humboldt Harbor and Crescent City in northern California. Congress appropriated $148,000 to launch the project, an impressive sum at the time, but one that would prove woefully inadequate.

In an attempt to stretch these federal dollars as far as possible, government officials decided to hire a single contractor to build the first eight lights, seven of them in California and one in Oregon. Unfortunately, the savings that might have been realized through this approach never got beyond the door of the U.S. Treasury. Through a corrupt paper-shuffling scheme, the contract was given to an unscrupulous Treasury Department official who understood nothing about the construction of lighthouses. He had no intention of building them himself and quickly sold the contract to a Baltimore firm, reaping a handsome profit in the process.

The company that ended up with the contract was a partnership of Francis Kelly and Francis Gibbons. The latter was a veteran lighthouse engineer who had built the Bodie Island Lighthouse on the Outer Banks of North Carolina. Kelly and Gibbons loaded up the sailing ship *Oriole* with supplies and sent it off to California by way of Cape Horn at the southern tip of South America.

When the *Oriole* arrived at San Francisco late in 1852, Gibbons's construction crew began work immediately on the Alcatraz

Alcatraz Light Station as it looked during the Civil War era—notice the stacked munitions.
National Archives

Island Lighthouse. Gibbons believed he and his men could build several lighthouses at once and that the work could be done faster and more efficiently in stages. So once the foundation was finished on Alcatraz, he moved part of his crew to Fort Point, where they prepared the site and started laying a second foundation. Hopping from place to place in this way, Gibbons's workers had four lighthouses standing within ten months. Then disaster struck.

In August 1853 the *Oriole* set sail from San Francisco to the mouth of the Columbia River, where work was scheduled to begin on a fifth lighthouse at Cape Disappointment. Having no light to guide her, the ship struck shoals near the entrance of the river and began to take on water. Feverish efforts to save the vessel proved unsuccessful, and she sank, carrying all the remaining construction materials down with her. Fortunately, the ship's crew and its complement of lighthouse builders were rescued.

Gibbons and Kelly scrambled frantically to replace the lost materials. Within a few months the partners had commissioned another ship and stocked her with supplies so that work could resume. By redoubling their efforts, they were able to get the project back on schedule. In August 1854, one year after the sinking of the *Oriole*, the last brick was laid on the Point Loma Lighthouse. All eight of the contracted lighthouses were now complete.

Although rightfully proud of their accomplishments, Gibbons and Kelly were in for a shock, as were government inspectors and lighthouse officials. When the Fresnel lenses intended for the new light stations arrived by ship from Europe, it quickly became apparent that they would not fit in the lanterns atop the towers of any of the lighthouses. The lanterns and in some cases, the towers themselves, were too small to accommodate the prismatic lenses. Most of the lighthouses had to be renovated, and the towers at Point Conception and on the Farallon Islands had to be torn down and completely rebuilt. Gibbons and Kelly had contracted to build the lighthouses for $15,000 each. The cost of renovations and rebuilding, added to the cost incurred from the loss of the *Oriole*, doubtless more than wiped out any profit the Baltimore businessmen had hoped to make.

Despite all these difficulties, however, the new maritime lights were soon shining. The first western beacon in service was the one at Alcatraz where, on June 1, 1854, the keeper lit the lamp inside the sparkling new lens. A sheet of bright light reached out across the formerly dark waters of San Francisco Bay, ushering in a new and safer era of navigation in the West.

Eventually, major coastal and primary harbor lights marked important points and ports all along the California coast. Not all are still standing, and more than a few have been taken out of service and allowed to go dark. But a surprising number of the old lighthouses have survived—in some cases for more than a century—the ravages of earthquake, wind, and weather. Many of the old lights are still burning, offering guidance to any sailor on the sea.

How to Use This Guide

California boasts more than thirty standing light towers, and every one is worth a look. *Lighthouses of California* takes you to each accessible lighthouse and to some that simply can't be reached. It also takes a loving backward glance at California's "Lost Lights," beacons that once shined bright but were snuffed out long ago.

The book is divided into four sections: San Diego to Santa Barbara; Point Conception to Point Montara; Lights at the Golden Gate; and Point Reyes to Crescent City. Within each section, lighthouses are presented geographically. This arrangement should make it easier to plan your lighthouse outings—as should the directions, telephone contacts, and other travel information included at the end of each listing.

You should be able to visit the most attractive and historic lighthouses in one of the sections in a single long-weekend excursion. To help you select the lighthouses you want to visit, individual listings include advice in the form of simple symbols: 📖 for lighthouses that are especially historic—most of them are; 🚗 for lighthouses that are accessible by car, boat, or foot; 📷 for visitor-friendly lighthouses that are frequently open to the public and feature museums or similar attractions; and 📷 for lighthouses that make great pictures—most of them are quite photogenic. Some very interesting and historic lighthouses no longer exist, and those are designated with a 🏠. For added convenience every listing also includes an easy-to-read summary of key information on the lighthouse: location; date the light was established; tower height; elevation of the focal plane; type of optic; current status; characteristic; range; and, for all active lighthouses, the precise latitude and longitude of the beacon.

We hope you enjoy your California lighthouse adventure.

CHAPTER ONE:
SAN DIEGO TO SANTA BARBARA

I t should come as no surprise that lighthouses seem to be prime real estate for ghosts. That may be true in part because so many lighthouses—western ones in particular—are Victorian in style, giving them just the sort of look we often associate with the spectral and with things that go bump in the night. And because of their exposed locations, lighthouses certainly have more than their share of dark and stormy weather. Whether Victorian or not, the old, abandoned dwellings and tall towers, with their glowing lights, do have a distinctly ghostly feeling about them. Most are, in fact, quite old—a century or more—and have seen many generations of keepers. When stories are told about the keepers and the families who served at these isolated stations years ago, it is easy to imagine their spirits returning to haunt the places where they lived and worked so long.

More than one keeper of the Point Vicente Lighthouse has felt a chill run up and down his spine at night—especially when the station's ladylike ghost puts in an appearance. As with most light-house ghosts, this one is associated with a tragic story: According to legend, the lady's lover had drowned in a shipwreck, and she walked the grounds of the light station incessantly, waiting for him to rejoin her. For decades, it seemed, the faithful lady drifted over the station grounds, sometimes almost nightly. Keepers and visitors would look out across the station property and there she would be, an indistinct shape floating just above the ground. Some said she wore a flowing white gown.

The mystery was solved by a young assistant keeper with an exceptionally quick and skeptical mind. He took careful note of the lady's habits. She appeared only at night and most often when the station's powerful rotating beacon moved in her direction. She had a particular fondness for nights when there was a light fog. The Point Vicente assistant keeper and amateur detective concluded that the feminine ghost was the work of slight imperfections in the third-order Fresnel lens in the lantern room atop the 67-foot tower. As the lens rotated, it refracted light toward the ground in a confusion of arcs. If the refractions came together in just the right way and found a patch of fog, the "lady" appeared. Despite the sensibleness of this explanation, most visitors prefer to believe a ghostly lady still walks the station grounds. And perhaps she does.

Some lighthouses are themselves ghosts. After serving faith-
fully for decades—sometimes a hundred years or more—they were
abandoned and allowed to fall into ruin. Other outmoded or no-
longer-needed lighthouses were intentionally razed to make room
for new government structures. Still others were sold as surplus
property to private enterprises for use as yacht clubs, restaurants,
and storage houses. California has more than its share of "ghost"
lighthouses—historic structures that now exist only in memory.

Your California lighthouse adventure should include at least a
few of these maritime jewels, "lost lights" such as Ballast Point
Lighthouse and the site of the old Point Hueneme Lighthouse. The
best of the still-standing lights in this region may be the old and
new Point Loma Lighthouse near San Diego, but don't miss the
Point Vicente, Point Fermin, and Los Angeles Harbor Lighthouses in
the City of Angels. You'll have to plan ahead and take a boat, but
the Anacapa Island Lighthouse may be the finest and best
preserved island light station in the West. Just getting to it is an
adventure in itself.

Guarded by a century-old,
iron-skeleton tower, this
Coast Guard light station
looks out toward the
Pacific from Point Loma.

Visitors to the Cabrillo National Monument near San Diego have a real treat in store: a chance to tour the West's oldest still-standing lighthouse. Although the Old Point Loma lantern has been dark for more than a century, the building remains in excellent condition and looks much the way it did when it first brightened the southern California coast during the 1850s. The old station provides a link to California's storied past and to the earliest efforts to light America's Pacific seaboard.

According to legend, Point Loma was named for a Russian girl who survived a shipwreck on these rugged shores only to be murdered later by an amorous local man whose attentions she had spurned. While this tragic tale has its attractions, the name probably derives from the Portuguese word for "light." It is believed that hundreds of years ago, when California was still part of Spain's colonial empire, soldiers built fires on lofty Point Loma to help royal supply ships reach harbor safely. Following acquisition of California by the United States in 1848, the government selected this same dramatic headland as the likeliest site for a lighthouse to mark the way to San Diego.

Francis Gibbons, who built many of the West's earliest light-houses, brought his crew of masons and laborers here during spring 1854; the work on the lighthouse was not completed until late the following year. Built of locally quarried sandstone, and brick brought by ship from Monterey, the combination Cape Cod–style dwelling and 46-foot tower ended up costing Uncle Sam a whopping $30,000. Despite what seemed a hefty price at the time, the struc-ture was not constructed according to specifications. When its first-order Fresnel lens arrived by sailing ship from France, workers could not fit it into the narrow lantern at the top of the tower. Instead, they substituted a third-order lens.

Worse problems lay ahead for the lighthouse. Although the station's third-order lens was less powerful than the one intended for it, the 462-foot elevation of the light made it visible from a distance of over 40 miles. That same extraordinary elevation, however, all too often placed the beacon above the low-lying clouds and fog banks that often enveloped the point. Mariners on the decks of ships below the clouds and fog could barely see the light if, indeed, they could see it at all. So, in 1891, only thirty-six years after its lamps were first lit, the Old Point Loma Light was deactivated, and a skeleton tower, built at a lower, more practical elevation, took its place.

TO SEE THE LIGHT: From Interstate 5 in San Diego, follow Catalina Boulevard (Route 209) to Cabrillo Memorial Drive through Fort Rosecrans National Cemetery to Cabrillo National Monument. Having refitted the light with a classical lens and furnished the dwelling much as it might have looked when its first keepers lived there, the Park Service maintains the Old Point Loma Light as a museum. For monument hours and other information, call (619) 557–5450.

Location: San Diego

Established: 1855

Tower height: 46 feet

Elevation of the focal plane: 462 feet

Optic: Fresnel lens (third order)

Status: Deactivated in 1891

Note: Oldest standing lighthouse in the West

(NEW) POINT LOMA LIGHT

Since fog often obscured the original Point Loma beacon, government maritime officials decided to build a second lighthouse at a lower, more practical elevation. Completed in 1891, the new Point Loma Light consists of a 70-foot, iron-skeleton tower and a separate two-story keeper's residence. A white cylinder centered between the tower's braced iron legs allows access to the lantern room. The original third-order Fresnel lens placed here in 1891 focused the light until 2002, when it was replaced by a modern optic. A horn at the base of the tower alerts vessels when fog shrouds the point.

Iron-skeleton towers like this one are rare on the West Coast of the United States. The technology for building them was developed in the eastern United States during the mid-nineteenth century. With their open-sided walls and stout iron bracing, these towers were designed to withstand extreme weather conditions, especially storm winds and high water. The nation's first iron-skeleton light tower, built on Minot's Ledge near Boston during the late 1840s, collapsed in a storm killing two assistant keepers.

TO SEE THE LIGHT: From Interstate 5 in San Diego, follow Catalina Boulevard (Route 209) to Cabrillo Memorial Drive through to Cabrillo National Monument. Located on an active Coast Guard installation, the station is closed to the public, but can be enjoyed from the monument parking area and from the road leading to the popular tidal pools. The monument has on display the third-order Fresnel lens that produced the Point Loma Lighthouse beacon until 2002. For monument hours and other information, call (619) 557–5450.

Location: San Diego

Established: 1891

Tower height: 70 feet

Elevation of the focal plane: 88 feet

Optic: Fresnel lens (modern)

Status: Active

Characteristic: Flashes white every 15 seconds

Range: 22 miles

Position: 32° 39' 54
117° 14' 34

Note: Located on an active Coast Guard facility

BALLAST POINT LIGHTHOUSE

A two-story Victorian structure similar in style to the lovely Point Fermin Lighthouse near Los Angeles, the Ballast Point Lighthouse was said by many to be among the most beautiful buildings in the West. Built in 1890, the combination tower and dwelling graced the point until 1961, when the station was removed to make room for a submarine base.

Those lucky enough to have seen it can recall the elegant detailing that made the Ballast Point Lighthouse a thing of beauty. It was highly functional, too. Its light, focused by a classic fifth-order Fresnel lens, guided countless ships to the safety of San Diego Harbor. While a simple automated light near here still guides vessels into San Diego Bay, the fine old lighthouse has been gone for nearly half a century.

Had the Ballast Point Lighthouse survived a few more years, it might never have been torn down. The 1960s were a time when Americans were focused on the future and, perhaps, placed less value than what they should have on historic architecture. Nowadays, such an elegant old buildings like this one would be saved from the wrecking ball.

TO SEE THE LIGHT: The lighthouse is gone, but the automated light can be seen from various points along the San Diego waterfront.

Location: San Diego

Established: 1890

Status: Deactivated and destroyed in 1961

Note: Razed to make room for a submarine base

LONG BEACH HARBOR LIGHT

Location: Los Angeles

Established: 1949

Tower height: 42 feet

Elevation of the focal
plane: 50 feet

Optic: Modern

Status: Active

Characteristic: Flashes
white every 15 seconds

Range: 20 miles

Position: 33° 43' 24
118° 11' 12

Note: Has been described
as the "Robot Light"

One could hardly imagine a less romantic edifice than the blocky, concrete structure marking the San Pedro Middle Breakwater in Los Angeles, but believe it or not, this is a lighthouse. Built half a century ago at a time when modernist architects thought in terms of the purely functional, it is indeed a radical departure from the old stone dwellings and towers built by Francis Gibbons. Ultramodern even by today's standards, it looks a bit like a space invader from a low-budget, 1950s science fiction movie. No doubt, that is why Los Angeles children know it as the "Robot Light."

Supported by six cylindrical columns made of cement cast into huge molds, the 42-foot-high rectangular tower is designed to with-stand both earthquakes and high winds. When the light went into operation in 1949, its functions were monitored and controlled electronically from the nearby Los Angeles Harbor Light. Nowadays, computers keep tabs on the light and relay commands to its airport-style beacon.

While not uncommon, automated lighthouses were still the exception when the Long Beach Harbor Light was established around the middle of the twentieth century. During the latter half of the century however, one light-house after another was automated by the U.S. Coast Guard and their keepers retired or were assigned to other duties. Now all of America's lighthouses are automated.

TO SEE THE LIGHT: Located at the end of the San Pedro Middle Breakwater, the Long Beach Harbor Light cannot be reached easily from shore and is off-limits to the public. However, the blocky tower and its light can be seen from numerous points along the coast.

Bob and Sandra Shanklin, The Lighthouse People

Rising more than seventy feet above the Pacific, the Romanesque Los Angeles Harbor Lighthouse has anchored the far end of the San Pedro Harbor Breakwater since 1913. Despite gales, earthquakes, and even a brush with a U.S. Navy battleship, the old tower has remained solid and functional since its construction in 1913. Its distinctive vertical black stripes and flashing green light are familiar sights to sailors entering the harbor and boaters enjoying the waters off Los Angeles.

Keepers lived here full time until the station was automated in 1973. The Coast Guard replaced the

Bob and Sandra Shanklin, The Lighthouse People

original fourth-order Fresnel lens with a modern optic when the facility was converted to solar power during the 1980s. The Los Angeles Maritime Museum in San Pedro now proudly displays the original 3,000-pound classic lens.

TO SEE THE LIGHT: Somewhat resembling a column from an ancient temple, the Los Angeles Harbor Lighthouse is best seen from the deck of a boat or ferry. For information on the Santa Catalina Ferry, which passes by the light, call (800) 360–1212. The tower can also be seen from Pacific Avenue and from Point Fermin City Park, where visitors can also enjoy the Point Fermin Lighthouse. Located nearby at the lower end of Sixth Street in San Pedro, the Los Angeles Maritime Museum features informative lighthouse exhibits and is well worth a visit. Call (310) 548–7618.

Location: Los Angeles

Established: 1913

Tower height: 69 feet

Elevation of the focal plane: 73 feet

Optic: Solar-powered modern

Status: Active

Characteristic: Flashes green every 15 seconds

Range: 18 miles

Position: 33° 42' 30
118° 15' 06

Note: Also known as the Angels Gate Lighthouse

POINT FERMIN LIGHTHOUSE

No longer in operation, the Point Fermin Lighthouse remains a venerable landmark. Built in 1874 with highly durable redwood, its Victorian-era Italianate styling and decorative gingerbread make it an architectural delight. Rising through the middle of the pitched roof, a square tower supports a lantern so small it almost goes unnoticed.

One might think this unusual structure unique, but not so. To cut costs, government engineers often used the same general set of plans to build more than one lighthouse, as was the case with the Point Fermin and its sister lighthouse at Point Hueneme near Oxnard. Unfortunately, the original Point Hueneme Lighthouse was torn down at the beginning of World War II, but two very similar buildings remain standing at the East Brother Island Light Station in San Francisco Bay, and at Hereford Inlet in New Jersey. Not coincidentally, all these lighthouses were completed in 1874.

If not for the efforts of a small group of history-minded preservationists, the Point Fermin Lighthouse might have suffered the same fate as its twin at Point Hueneme. The fourth-order Fresnel lens that once shone here was removed during World War II when the structure was pressed into service as a coastal watchtower. During the decades that followed, the station's lantern was removed and the building itself fell into such disrepair that the government planned to demolish it. But local lighthouse lovers stepped in to save the old lighthouse. Its lantern replaced, the old lighthouse now graces Point Fermin City Park.

Interestingly, Point Fermin still has a navigational beacon. It shines from a pole not far from the original light station. Mariners within 13 miles of the point can see its light flash once every ten seconds.

TO SEE THE LIGHT: Now maintained as a museum by the City of Los Angeles, the lighthouse is open to the public for a few hours each Sunday; the hours may be extended in the near future. To reach Point Fermin City Park, follow Route 110 to Gaffney Street and turn north. The lighthouse is located on Paseo Del Mar, west of Pacific Avenue. The park offers an excellent place to view the Los Angeles Harbor Light, as well.

Location: Los Angeles

Established: 1874

Tower height: 30 feet

Elevation of the focal plane: 100 feet

Status: Deactivated in 1942

Note: Extraordinary architecture

POINT VICENTE LIGHT

S ituated on a cliff high above the blue Pacific and surrounded by graceful palms, the sparkling white Point Vicente tower fits everyone's romantic image of a southern California lighthouse. In fact, film crews have used it as the backdrop for countless movie and television scenes. Built in 1926 near the edge of a rocky cliff more than a hundred feet above the ocean, the 67-foot cylindrical tower is crowned by a handsome lantern with cross-hatched windows. The original third-order Fresnel lens still shines each night, producing a powerful 1.1 million candlepower flash every twenty seconds. It can be seen from 24 miles away.

Naturally, this quintessential lighthouse has a resident ghost. The ladylike phantom appears only on foggy nights and is said to be the former lover of a sailor who died in a shipwreck on Point Vicente. Skeptics say she is nothing more than an optical illusion created by stray refractions of the station's lens, but that should not deter romantic souls from enjoying the legend and perhaps casting an eye about when fog rolls across the point.

Perhaps Point Vicente's feminine ghost took a holiday during World War II. While fighting in the Pacific raged, the station's Fresnel was blacked out to prevent Japanese submarines from using it to help them track down vulnerable American freighters. A smaller, less brilliant light served Point Vicente until the war was over, at which time the original Fresnel lens was once more placed in service. Incidentally, the Point Vicente's lens is considerably older than the lighthouse itself. The lens had been used in an Alaska lighthouse for nearly forty years before being brought to California in 1926.

TO SEE THE LIGHT: The lighthouse is located north of Marineland off Palos Verdes Drive. A fine view of the light can be had from the grounds of the nearby Palos Verdes Interpretive Center; call (310) 377–5370. Exhibits recount the history of the lighthouse and explore the natural history of the Palos Verdes peninsula.

Location: Los Angeles

Established: 1926

Tower height: 67 feet

Elevation of the focal plane: 185 feet

Optic: Fresnel lens (third order)

Status: Active

Characteristic: Flashes twice every 20 seconds

Range: 24 miles

Position: 33° 44' 30
118° 24' 36

Note: Said to be haunted

POINT HUENEME LIGHT

An identical twin of the ornate Point Fermin Lighthouse once stood in Oxnard, northwest of Los Angeles, marking the heavily traveled Santa Barbara Channel. Both structures consisted of a square, 30-foot-high redwood tower rising through the roof of an Italianate residence. Not only did these stations look exactly alike, but they came to life on the same day, showing their lights for the first time on December 1, 1874. A matched pair of fourth-order Fresnel lenses focused their beacons. Their lights were not identical, however: The Point Hueneme station flashed white, while the Point Fermin displayed alternate white and red flashes.

Also unlike its twin, the original Point Hueneme Lighthouse did not survive the ravages of time. Deteriorating from repeated battering by storms, it was sold to private owners in 1941 and eventually torn down. A far-less attractive, though nonetheless effective, square 48-foot-high concrete tower took its place. The existing tower reflects the art deco styling of a number of lighthouses built during the same period in Alaska.

TO SEE THE LIGHT: Located on an active naval installation, the Point Hueneme Light tower is off-limits to the public. Its light remains active, however, and can be seen from many points along the nearby coast. A reasonably close-up view can be had by walking north along a path leading from the beach near the Hueneme fishing pier.

Location: Oxnard

Established: 1874

Tower height: 48 feet

Elevation of the focal plane: 52 feet

Optic: Modern

Status: Active

Characteristic: Flashes white every 30 seconds

Range: 20 miles

Position: 34° 08' 43
119° 12' 36

Note: Original wooden lighthouse destroyed

The Point Hueneme keeper (front row, left of center) hosts a gathering, likely of construction workers and lighthouse service personnel, around the turn of the century.
U.S. Coast Guard

From a distance southern California's beautiful Channel Islands seem placid, but their jagged rocks have torn apart countless ships. The Spanish treasure ship *San Sebastion* wrecked here in 1784, dumping its shipment of gold doubloons into the surf. In 1853 the steamer *Winfield Scott* slammed into Anacapa Island, stranding 250 passengers for several weeks without food or shelter.

Government officials had long recognized the need for a light to warn mariners of the dangers here, but until the twentieth century, few believed a lighthouse could be built on the island's rugged, almost perpendicular, cliffs. In 1912 the project was finally attempted, and after considerable effort, a light station was established on Anacapa Island. Equipped with an automated, acetylene lamp, its iron-skeleton tower stood near the spot where the *Winfield Scott* had run onto the rocks nearly sixty years earlier.

In 1932, the Lighthouse Service assigned resident keepers to the station and built a new, 55-foot-tall masonry tower. Although not as tall, the tower looks much like the one at Point Vicente near Los Angeles. The height of the cliffs placed its light 277 feet above the ocean, from which elevation its third-order beacon could be seen from 20 miles away. Always difficult to supply, especially with fresh water, the station was automated in 1969. A modern lens replaced the original Fresnel in 1991.

TO SEE THE LIGHT: The Anacapa Lighthouse is now part of Channel Islands National Park, one of the nation's foremost scenic wonders; call (805) 658–5700. Visits to Anacapa and other islands are available through park concessionaires in Ventura; call (805) 642–1393. To reach the park's visitor center from U.S. Highway 101 in Ventura, follow Victoria Avenue, Olivas Park Drive, and Spinnaker Drive to Ventura Harbor. The original Anacapa Island third-order Fresnel lens is on display at the center.

Location: Anacapa Island

Established: 1912

Tower height: 55 feet

Elevation of the focal plane: 277 feet

Optic: Modern

Status: Active

Characteristic: Flashes twice every 60 seconds

Range: 20 miles

Position: 34° 00' 56
119° 21' 34

Note: Recently underwent a $350,000 restoration

SANTA BARBARA LIGHT

A simple, white tower on a Coast Guard base just west of Santa Barbara now serves in place of the city's historic lighthouse, destroyed during a major earthquake in 1925. Among the first lighthouses in the West, the original structure was built by contractor George Nagle for a modest $8,000. Like many early California lighthouses, it consisted of a Cape Cod–style dwelling with a tower rising through its roof. For many years the original lighthouse was the home of Julia Williams, one of America's most famous lighthouse keepers. She tended the Santa Barbara Light for more than forty years, and it is said she spent only two nights away from the station during that time.

TO SEE THE LIGHT: The existing automated light tower is closed to the public. However, the flashing beacon can be seen from the water and a number of points along the shore.

Location: Santa Barbara

Established: 1856

Tower height: 25 feet

Elevation of the focal plane: 142 feet

Optic: Modern

Status: Active

Characteristic: Flashes white every 10 seconds

Range: 25 miles

Position: 34° 23' 48
119° 43' 24

Note: Historic lighthouse destroyed in 1925 earthquake

National Archives

CHAPTER TWO:
POINT CONCEPTION TO POINT MONTARA

For travelers who love beautiful scenery, the central coast of California is an earthly paradise. A bold range of geologically young mountains meets the planet's oldest and most extensive ocean.

Whether seen from land or water, this coast is enchanting, but mariners know it is not just a place of beauty. Danger lurks along these shores. Colonial-era Spanish treasure ships, bearing silk and spices from the Orient, crossed 5,000 miles of the open Pacific to reach California, but were seldom so threatened as when they approached the coast. Just as they are today, California's headlands were often draped in fog and all but invisible. A captain's first warning of landfall might be the grinding and splintering of his hull on stone. Or a storm might blow up suddenly and send his ship hurtling out of control toward the rocks. Many of these ships and their crews simply vanished, never to be seen or heard from again. No one knows how many Spanish wrecks may lie in the waters off California. The carnage off this coast has continued right up into our own times. Even with coastal lights, the best charts, and the finest navigational instruments to guide them, sailors still get lost here.

Perhaps the worst maritime disaster in California history took place on September 8, 1923, when a fleet of fourteen U.S. Navy destroyers took a wrong turn off Point Arguello. Pushing south from San Francisco to San Diego, the fleet was under the overall command of Captain Edward Watson, who ordered his ships to maintain a precise military formation, running one behind the other about two minutes apart. Despite a thick fog cloaking both the sea and the shoreline just to the east, the fleet was making good time, steaming steadily ahead at twenty knots.

In order to maintain a uniform distance from the shore, Captain Watson intended to turn his vessels to the east once they had passed Point Conception, where the California coastline changes course. This shift in the shoreline is marked by a pair of lights on Point Arguello and Point Conception. Peering into the darkness, Captain Watson had seen neither of the two beacons. Growing impatient, he became convinced that he had missed the lights in the heavy fog and that the flotilla was now well to the south of Point Conception.

Just as he was about to give the order that would turn his destroyers to the east, supposedly into the Santa Barbara Channel,

Watson received a surprising message from the *Delphy*, the fleet's lead vessel. The *Delphy*'s navigator reported receiving the signal of the radio beacon on Point Arguello. The flotilla commander was momentarily puzzled. If the report was accurate and the signal was the one from Point Arguello, then the *Delphy* and the rest of the fleet were still well to the north of Point Conception. The captain decided his navigator must be mistaken. For one thing, he had received a second radio signal that seemed to indicate the destroyers had cleared Conception. For another, Captain Watson was an old sailor who trusted his instinct for dead reckoning more than any navigational contraption. He gave the order.

Unfortunately, the second signal had been false and the captain's reckoning was mistaken. Shortly after the ships began their turn to the east, chaos broke out at a place called Honda, a mile or so north of the Point Arguello Lighthouse. Metal screamed and ruptured boilers hissed as the *Delphy* and, one after another, the *Lee*, *Young*, *Woodbury*, *Chauncey*, *Nicholas*, and *Fuller* slammed into the shore, striking the rocks at approximately two-minute intervals.

Point Arguello Lighthouse keepers Gotford Olson, Arvel Settles, and Jesse Mygrants could hear the drumming of engines as the destroyers steamed toward their doom. The keepers pulled many sailors out of the surf. Injured men were treated at the lighthouse. Later, the keepers would receive commendations for their efforts.

In all, seven ships went aground that night. Another seven managed to turn away in time and run for safety. Twenty-three sailors lost their lives and many others were injured. In memory of the ships and men lost in this tragic mishap, a memorial anchor was placed at Honda on a bluff overlooking the site of the wrecks.

Countless conventional vessels and the mariners aboard them owe an enormous debt to the lighthouses along the California coast. In fact, so do the rest of us, because neither the West nor the nation as a whole could have prospered without them. California's lighthouses still have much to offer for those who approach them from the landward side as well. This is especially true along the central coast where several historic lights are open to visitors, such as the Point Pinos Lighthouse in Pacific Grove, which once played host to *Treasure Island* author Robert Louis Stevenson. South of Monterey is the Point Sur Lighthouse, with one of the most spectacular settings in the West. North of Santa Cruz are the Pigeon Point and Point Montara Lighthouses; both serve as hostelries with bargain accommodations as well as historical interest and natural beauty.

POINT CONCEPTION LIGHT

Bob and Sandra Shanklin,
The Lighthouse People

At Point Conception, ships headed along the California coast must change course, either northward toward San Francisco or eastward toward Los Angeles. Here colliding ocean currents generate some of the worst weather in America, causing experienced seamen to compare Point Conception to South America's notoriously stormy Cape Horn. And well they should. The crushed hulls of wrecked vessels—eighteenth-century Spanish sailing ships and more recent American steamers—litter the churning waters off this dramatic angle of land.

Aware of Point Conception's importance and nightmarish reputation, the U.S. government chose its isolated cliff tops as the site for one of the West's earliest light stations. Built with great difficulty in 1854, the lighthouse was beset with problems from the start. Workmanship of the brick and mortar structure was shoddy, and the combination tower and dwelling began to fall apart almost as soon as it was finished. Worse, the tower was too small for the first-order Fresnel lens assigned to it. Finally, the contractors had to tear the whole thing down and start over again. Then, when the keepers installed the big lens, they discovered that several key parts of the lighting apparatus were missing, and new ones had to be ordered from France.

Once the station finally became operational in 1856, it quickly became apparent that the tower had been built too high on the cliffs. Fog and low-lying clouds frequently obscured the light. Weakened by repeated gales and earthquakes, the building was finally abandoned in 1882 in favor of a better-constructed lighthouse built at a more practical elevation of about 130 feet above sea level. The 2-foot-thick, 52-foot-high brick and granite walls have aged well. The lighthouse remains as solid as ever, and the station's original 10-foot-high, first-order lens remains in place. Nowadays, however, the Point Conception beacon is produced by a modern optic mounted on the railing of the lantern gallery.

TO SEE THE LIGHT: Nearly impossible to approach from land or sea, the station is closed to the public.

Location: Point Conception

Established: 1856

Tower height: 52 feet

Elevation of the focal plane: 133 feet

Optic: Modern

Status: Active

Characteristic: Flashes white every 30 seconds

Range: 20 miles

Position: 34° 26' 54
120° 28' 12

Note: First-order Fresnel lens remains in the lantern

POINT ARGUELLO LIGHTHOUSE

On the evening of September 8, 1923, seven U.S. Navy destroyers slammed into the fog-shrouded coast within shouting distance of the Point Arguello Lighthouse, with disastrous results. While its light and radio beacons failed to prevent this calamity, the lighthouse's beacons have no doubt saved countless other ships from a similar fate. Completed in 1901, the station's squat 28-foot-tall tower stood on a cliff more than 100 feet above the sea. In good weather its fixed white beacon, produced by a fourth-order Fresnel lens, could be seen from many miles out in the Pacific. Isolated and difficult to supply, Point Arguello was among the first Pacific coast lights to be automated. Decommissioned in 1934, the lighthouse was razed and replaced by an aero-marine beacon on an iron-skeleton tower.

TO SEE THE LIGHT: As part of Vandenberg Air Force Base, Point Arguello is closed to the public. The best way to see the light is from the sea. However, Amtrak passengers riding past Point Arguello may catch a glimpse of this remote and rather unglamorous light station.

Location: Lompoc

Established: 1901

Status: Deactivated in 1934 and later demolished

Note: Site of 1923 naval disaster

National Archives

SAN LUIS OBISPO LIGHTHOUSE

Although the lovely, old Spanish town of San Luis Obispo had one of the best harbors in southern California, it was among the last West Coast ports to receive a lighthouse. Regional political squabbling blocked congressional appropriations until the late 1880s, when funds finally became available.

Built on an isolated point on the west side of San Luis Obispo Bay, the station was ready for service by June 1890. It consisted of a distinctly Victorian two-story residence with a square, 40-foot tower rising from one corner, and a fog signal building with a 10-inch steam whistle. A fourth-order Fresnel lens produced the beacon, which had a focal plane 116 feet above sea level. Because there was no road leading to the point—there still is not—U.S. Lighthouse Service supply steamers made regular calls at the San Luis Obispo station.

The light was automated in 1974, and about a year later the old lighthouse lost its job to a cylindrical structure built just to the east. The new, far less scenic tower boasts a powerful, modern optic producing a flashing white signal that can be seen from 20 miles at sea. The Fresnel lens that served so long in the lighthouse has been moved to a museum in town.

After the San Luis Obispo Light was automated and moved out of the tower to an adjacent structure, the old lighthouse fell into disrepair. The original station buildings might have been torn down save for the efforts of local preservationists. A group known as the San Luis Obispo Keepers is restoring the lighthouse for use as an educational facility. When their work is complete, the Keepers will have a truly historic property on their hands.

The San Luis Obispo Lighthouse was the last of a series of combination light towers and dwellings built in a distinctly Victorian style by the old U.S. Lighthouse Service. Earlier California lighthouses at Ballast Point near San Diego, Point Fermin near Los Angeles, Point Hueneme near Oxnard, and on East Brother Island in San Francisco Bay were built using a similar set of plans. Of these, only the lighthouses at Point Fermin and East Brother Island still stand.

TO SEE THE LIGHT: The lighthouse is located near the Diablo Canyon Nuclear Power Plant and has been long off-limits to visitors. However, at press time, local preservationists were restoring the historic structure, and have plans to open it to the public. The station's Fresnel lens can now be seen at the San Luis Obispo County Historical Museum at 696 Monterey Street; call (805) 543–0638. The San Luis Obispo Conservancy occasionally organizes day hikes to the lighthouse; call (805) 541–8735.

Location: San Luis Obispo
Established: 1890
Tower height: 40 feet
Elevation of the focal plane: 116 feet
Optic: Fresnel lens (fourth order) removed
Status: Deactivated in 1975
Note: Historic structures under restoration

PIEDRAS BLANCAS LIGHT

utomation transformed this once handsome lighthouse into an ugly duckling. During a 1949 renovation its lovely old lantern was lopped off and a rotating, airport-style beacon was set atop the decapitated tower to do the work of the original first-order Fresnel lens.

When completed in 1875, the cone-shaped brick tower stood 90 feet tall on a grassy knoll that boosted its light to an elevation of more than 140 feet. With its ornate gallery and crown-like lantern, the tower looked a bit like a giant, elegantly carved, ivory chess rook. The unattractive modern beacon that serves here today is no less powerful, and can be seen from up to 21 miles out in the Pacific.

Location: North of
San Simeon

Established: 1875

Tower height: 74 feet

Elevation of the focal
plane: 142 feet

Optic: Modern

Status: Active

Characteristic: Flashes
white every 10 seconds

Range: 21 miles

Position: 35° 39' 56
121° 17' 04

Note: Site of major
elephant seal colony

Despite its appearance, the old lighthouse is a favorite of tourists who visit the area to see the Hearst Castle in San Simeon or to view the impressive colony of elephant seals that wallow on the beaches near the tower. The seals are enormous, so much so that lying buried in the sand, they can be mistaken for large boulders.

TO SEE THE LIGHT: The lighthouse is located on Highway 1 about 1 mile north of San Simeon. Although closed to the public, the tower can be viewed from the roadside. The elephant seals can be viewed from a large parking area not far from the lighthouse. The station's nicely restored first-order lens is housed in a handsome lantern-like structure on Main Street in the nearby town of Cambria.

POINT SUR LIGHT

A t Big Sur the churning Pacific makes relentless war on a chain of coastal mountains. The same natural forces—weather and geology—responsible for this scenic spectacle have also made it a very dangerous place for ships. Countless seafaring vessels—and one dirigible—have been lost here. But since 1889, the powerful beacon of the Point Sur Lighthouse has warned mariners to keep away.

It was once thought impossible to build a light station on Big Sur's precipitous cliffs, but the U.S. Lighthouse Service took up the challenge during the late 1880s. Before construction could begin, workers had to lay tracks for a special railroad car to carry materials and supplies to the rugged sandstone mountain known as Point Sur. The project took two years of hard work and more than $100,000 to complete.

The station consisted of a 40-foot-tall granite tower atop the cliffs, and a collection of dwellings and other buildings nearer the water. Keepers found the lighthouse almost as hard to maintain as it had been to build. Every night they had to trudge up the 395 steps leading to the tower to tend the light. The station was finally automated in 1972, all but eliminating the need for the long daily climb. At that time a rotating aero-beacon replaced the original first-order Fresnel lens.

TO SEE THE LIGHT: The lighthouse can be seen from several places along Highway 1 on the way from Monterey to Big Sur. A turnout near the crest of lofty Hurricane Ridge, about 15 miles south of Carmel, provides a clear, though distant, view of the lighthouse. The station's sizeable first-order Fresnel lens is now impressively displayed at the Allen Knight Maritime Museum near Fisherman's Wharf in Monterey; call (831) 373-2469.

Location: Big Sur

Established: 1889

Tower height: 48 feet

Elevation of the focal plane: 273 feet

Optic: Modern

Status: Active

Characteristic: Flashes white every 15 seconds

Range: 25 miles

Position: 36° 18' 24
121° 54' 06

Note: Near site of 1935 dirigible crash

POINT PINOS LIGHT

Location: Pacific Grove

Established: 1855

Tower height: 43 feet

Elevation of the focal
plane: 89 feet

Optic: Fresnel lens
(third order)

Status: Active

Characteristic: White
occulting

Range: 17 miles

Position: 36° 38' 00
121° 56' 00

Note: Oldest active light
in California

Now surrounded by a lush golf course, the West Coast's oldest active lighthouse is leased by the Coast Guard to the Pacific Grove Museum of Natural History, which uses it as a maritime museum. Like many other early California lighthouses built during the 1850s by contractor Francis Gibbons, this one consists of a Cape Cod–style, stone keeper's residence with a conical brick tower rising through its roof. Originally granite, the structure was covered over with reinforced concrete following the severe earthquake that devastated San Francisco and much of the central California coast in 1906. The third-order Fresnel lens in place here since 1855 still shines.

Counted among the West's historic treasures, the old lighthouse has played host to many notables such as John Steinbeck and Robert Louis Stevenson. The station's first keeper, former gold rush miner Charles Layton, died in a shoot-out with the notorious bandito Anastasio Garcia. Layton's wife then took over as keeper.

TO SEE THE LIGHT: Located on Lighthouse Avenue between Sunset Drive and Asilomar Avenue at the far western end of Pacific Grove, the lighthouse is open to the public on Saturday and Sunday afternoons. For more information call the Pacific Grove Museum of Natural History at (831) 648–3116.

SANTA CRUZ LIGHT

E stablished in 1869, the Santa Cruz Light guided lumber and lime freighters in and out of the harbor. Laura Heacox, daughter of the station's first keeper, tended this light for nearly half a century. Its beacon darkened during World War II, the wood and brick lighthouse was torn down in 1948. The brick light tower seen here today was built in 1967 with private funds as a memorial to teenager Mark Abbott, who drowned nearby in a surfing accident. The building houses a surfing museum, while the navigational light in the tower continues to guide mariners.

TO SEE THE LIGHT: Follow West Cliff Drive in Santa Cruz to Lighthouse Point. The museum is free and open every afternoon except Tuesday; call (831) 420–6289.

Location: Santa Cruz

Established: 1869

Tower height: 39 feet

Elevation of the focal plane: 60 feet

Optic: Modern

Status: Active

Characteristic: Flashes white every 5 seconds

Range: 17 miles

Position: 36° 57' 06
122° 01' 36

Note: Built as a memorial for a drowned surfer

Nancy Pizzo

PIGEON POINT LIGHT

The Pigeon Point Light, some 50 miles south of San Francisco, shines out toward the Pacific from an elevation of nearly 150 feet. Little more than 40 feet of that height is provided by the point; the rest comes from the 115-foot brick tower. One of the tallest light towers on the Pacific Coast, it was built in 1872 with brick shipped around Cape Horn. The land, lighthouse, and huge first-order Fresnel lens cost the government approximately $20,000. While the big, polished-glass prismatic lens remains in the tower, a modern optic mounted on the gallery rail now focuses the powerful Pigeon Point beacon. Pigeon Point takes its name from the Yankee clipper *Carrier Pigeon*, wrecked here in 1853.

TO SEE THE LIGHT: Now open to the public as a hostelry, the station is located just off Highway 1 south of the small, bucolic town of Pescadero. The grounds are open year-round. Call (650) 879–0633. Southwest of Pigeon Point is the mostly ruined Ano Nuevo Lighthouse, built in 1872 and now part of a state nature preserve. Deactivated in 1948, this station is used by the University of California at Santa Cruz as a marine research facility.

Location: Pescadero

Established: 1872

Tower height: 115 feet

Elevation of the focal plane: 148 feet

Optic: Modern

Status: Active

Characteristic: Flashes white every 10 seconds

Range: 24 miles

Position: 37° 10' 54
122° 23' 36

Note: Named for a wrecked clipper

POINT MONTARA LIGHT

I n 1868 the steamer *Colorado* ran aground on a ledge near Point
Montara. Four years later the freighter *Acuelo* wrecked just below
the point, spilling into the sea a cargo of coal and iron worth at
least $150,000. The latter disaster led to the placement of a fog
signal on Point Montara in 1872. Nearly three decades would pass

before the Point Montara fog-signal station became a full-fledged lighthouse. A simple pole light, set up in 1900, served until 1912, when it was replaced by a wooden tower.

The existing 30-foot cast-iron tower was built at the edge of the rocky point in 1928. Its light shines out toward the Pacific from an elevation of 70 feet. The station's fourth-order Fresnel lens gave way to a modern optic in 1970.

Iron light towers like the one that now marks Point Montara were developed during the mid-nineteenth century for use at navigational stations where they would likely be exposed to harsh weather conditions. Easily moved, these adaptable structures were often built at foundries and shipped to their assigned locations, or they could be assembled on site by bolting together curved iron plates, as was the case at Point Montara.

TO SEE THE LIGHT: The lighthouse is located off Highway 1 about 25 miles south of San Francisco. Most of the station buildings, including the Victorian-style keeper's quarters, are now used as a youth hostel; call (650) 728–7177. Visitors are welcome to walk the grounds.

Location: Montara

Established: 1900

Tower height: 30 feet

Elevation of the focal plane: 70 feet

Optic: Modern

Status: Active

Characteristic: Flashes white every 5 seconds

Range: 15 miles

Position: 37° 32' 12
122° 31' 12

Note: Now a popular youth hostel

CHAPTER THREE:
LIGHTS AT THE GOLDEN GATE

I n 1848 the sharp eye of a worker building a sawmill on California's American River caught the glimmer of something shiny in a streambed. Bending over, he reached down and picked up the piece of yellow metal about the size of a pea. It was gold, and within a year, news of its discovery had reached the ears of poor but hopeful people all around the world. By 1849, thousands of ships bearing countless prospectors were dropping anchor in San Francisco Bay.

The gold rush quickly transformed a remote American territory into one of the nation's fastest growing and most prosperous states. It also alerted federal maritime officials to the desperate need for navigation lights in the West. The wreck of gold rush–era ships, such as the *Tennessee* (1851), *Winfield Scott* (1853), the *Carrier Pigeon* (1853), and, rather ironically, the *San Francisco* (1854), prodded Congress to appropriate money to establish light stations throughout the region.

Not surprisingly, this large-scale effort began with construction of a lighthouse near San Francisco, the epicenter of the gold rush. Completed in 1854, the Alcatraz (Pelican) Island Lighthouse guided vessels through the Golden Gate Strait to the city's bustling wharves. In time other beacons at Point Bonita, Fort Point, and elsewhere helped mariners find their way through the strait and to San Francisco Bay.

As many as ten different lighthouses once marked the strait, the shores of the bay, or the banks of the Sacramento River. Most are now gone, but even the towers that no longer stand have histories that are well worth remembering. Among the towers that have vanished is the Point Knox Light in San Francisco Bay, duty station of a legendary female keeper named Juliet Nichols; the Oakland Harbor Light, built in 1890, automated in 1966, and eventually sold for use as a restaurant; the Southhampton Shoal Light near Oakland; Mare Island Light at the junctions of the Sacramento, San Joaquin, and Napa Rivers; Roe Island Light in Suisan Bay; and the Carquinez Strait Light, which once guided vessels into the narrow passage above San Pablo Bay. All of these historic lighthouses are gone or have been converted to other uses, but we can celebrate them by visiting the California lighthouses that still stand. There is no better place to do this than San Francisco.

Tourists and residents alike consider the Bay area lighthouses a necessary part of the San Francisco experience. Indeed, no visit here would be complete without a tour of Alcatraz Island, with its famous beacon and prison, or a side trip to Point Bonita, with its graceful tower and miniature of the Golden Gate Bridge. These still-functioning historic treasures evoke California's rough and ready past as well as its rich maritime heritage.

The lantern room at East Brother Island Light overlooking San Francisco Bay.

FARALLON ISLANDS LIGHT

During the 1850s, when the U.S. government shouldered the daunting task of lighting the nation's Pacific coast, maritime officials decided to start with the most strategic and dangerous locations. Perhaps foremost among these were the nearly barren Farallon Islands, about 20 miles west of San Francisco. More than a few vessels had come to grief on the islands' rugged shores, and a powerful Farallon beacon would not only warn mariners but also point the way to the Golden Gate and the safe waters of San Francisco Bay beyond.

Built in 1853 by a construction crew consisting of failed gold rush prospectors and a mule named "Paddy," the lighthouse was never used. Like several other early California lighthouses, it proved too small to serve its purpose. When the station's first-order Fresnel lens arrived by ship from France, the bulky bronze and glass optic could not be wedged into the narrow tower. As a result, the original structure had to be torn down and rebuilt. The new, larger tower was not completed and its lens not installed until late in 1854. Finally, on January 1, 1855, the station's lamps were lit, and its powerful light began to shine out over the Pacific.

Early keepers at this station were caught in the middle of a bizarre "egg war." Poachers made large profits stealing eggs from the millions of seabirds nesting on South Farallon and other nearby islands. So large and lucrative were their hauls that greedy poachers fought with one another for gathering rights. When gunfire erupted, California lawmen stepped in and drove off the poachers.

One of the nation's most isolated lighthouses, the Farallon Islands station was automated in 1972. At the same time, the big, first-order Fresnel was exchanged for a modern optic.

TO SEE THE LIGHT: The seabird species that once provided eggs for gold rush breakfasts now find safe haven in the Farallon National Wildlife Refuge. The islands are protected and difficult to reach, but the Oceanic Society in San Francisco offers cruises that provide views of the lighthouse as well as the islands' abundant wildlife; call (800) 326–7491. The original Farallon first-order lens is now on display at the San Francisco Maritime National Historical Park near Fisherman's Wharf; call (415) 447–5000.

Location: South Farallon Island

Established: 1855

Tower height: 41 feet

Elevation of the focal plane: 358 feet

Optic: Modern

Status: Active

Characteristic: Flashes white every 15 seconds

Range: 20 miles

Position: 37° 41' 54
         123° 00' 06

Note: Site of infamous "egg war"

MILE ROCKS LIGHT

L ittle remains of the original caisson-style light station that once marked the dangerous rocks that rise from the Pacific about 1 mile from the entrance of the Golden Gate Strait, which links San Francisco Bay to the open ocean. In 1966 the Coast Guard removed the iron tower and lantern that had stood on the massive caisson since 1905, replacing it with a simple, automated beacon. Although the lighthouse is gone, the beacon remains a key navigational guidepost. The light is powered with batteries that are recharged by solar panels.

TO SEE THE LIGHT: The beacon can be seen from Lincoln Park in San Francisco. From Highway 1 (Presidio Boulevard) follow Geary Boulevard and Point Lobos Avenue to the park.

Location: San Francisco

Established: 1905

Tower height: 40 feet

Elevation of the focal plane: 49 feet

Optic: Modern

Status: Active

Characteristic: Flashes white every 5 seconds

Range: 15 miles

Position: 37° 47' 34
           122° 30' 37

Note: Marks the entrance to the Golden Gate Strait

Of the once impressive open-water Mile Rocks Lighthouse, little remains but the concrete foundation. Bob and Sandra Shanklin, The Lighthouse People

Built in 1901, the original Mile Rocks Lighthouse consisted of a series of cylinders stacked one atop the other. Herman Jaehne

FORT POINT LIGHTHOUSE

Completed in 1853, at about the same time as the original Alcatraz Island lighthouse, the Fort Point Lighthouse had an important job to do, that of marking the channel through the Golden Gate and into San Francisco Bay. Yet the lighthouse stood empty for more than a year while waiting for its third-order Fresnel lens to arrive from France. The lens though, was never installed and the tower's lamps never lit. Before the station could be placed in operation, the lighthouse was torn down to make way for the massive brick walls of Fort Winfield Scott. The Fresnel lens originally intended for Fort Point was shipped south for use in the Point Pinos Lighthouse on Monterey Bay, where it still shines today after more than 140 years.

While the three-story fortress was under construction, workers built a wooden light tower at the water's edge. By 1864 storm-driven Pacific waves threatened to sweep the tower away and undermine the foundations of the fort. To make way for a protective seawall, the lighthouse was torn down again. This time it was replaced by a 27-foot iron-skeleton tower perched like a giant seabird atop the fort's lofty parapet. The additional height made the light, focused by a rather modest fifth-order lens, easier for approaching seamen to see.

The station served its purpose for more than seven decades, until construction of the Golden Gate Bridge made it obsolete. The station's light was snuffed out for good in 1934. Towering 740 feet above the sea, the bridge itself is a mammoth lighthouse. From miles away mariners can see its lights and recognize the distinctive inverted arches of its supporting cables. Completed and opened to traffic in 1937, the bridge is one of the world's most recognizable structures.

TO SEE THE LIGHT: Approaching the Golden Gate Bridge from the south on U.S. Highway 101, take LAST SAN FRANCISCO EXIT, then follow Lincoln Boulevard and Long Avenue to Fort Point National Historical Site. Open daily except for major holidays, the old fort with its tiny lighthouse offers wonderful views of San Francisco and the Golden Gate Bridge. Call (415) 556–1693. Less scenic, although still operational, is the blocky, concrete Lime Point Lighthouse on the opposite side of the Golden Gate Strait. It can be viewed from behind a fence at the end of Sausalito's Fort Baker Road.

Location: San Francisco

Established: 1855

Tower height: 27 feet

Elevation of the focal plane: 110 feet

Optic: Fresnel lens (fifth order)

Status: Deactivated in 1934

Note: Stands on the wall of a nineteenth-century fort

ALCATRAZ ISLAND LIGHT

D erived from *alcatraces*—the Spanish word for "pelican"—the name "Alcatraz" now has a cold and forbidding ring to it, and no wonder. For years Alcatraz Island in San Francisco Bay was the home of Al Capone and many other notorious criminals. Here they served "hard-time" at a federal penitentiary made escape-proof by high concrete walls and the shark-infested waters of the bay.

In contrast mariners and lighthouse lovers have warm feelings toward the island, for it is home to the oldest major navigational light on the West Coast. Francis Gibbons built the island's original light-house, a Cape Cod–style dwelling with a short tower peeking just above its roof. The lamps inside its third-order Fresnel lens were first lit on the evening of June 1, 1854. At that time gold-hungry miners were still arriving by sea, and the Alcatraz Island beacon guided them into San Francisco Bay and on toward their respective destinies.

Location: San Francisco

Established: 1854

Tower height: 84 feet

Elevation of the focal plane: 214 feet

Optic: Modern

Status: Active

Characteristic: Flashes white every 5 seconds

Range: 22 miles

Position: 37° 49' 36
122° 25' 18

Note: Site of the West's first lighthouse

The great San Francisco earthquake of 1906 caused Alcatraz keeper B.F. Leeds to believe he was witnessing "the end of the world." Not so, but the shaking did end the career of the little Gibbons lighthouse. The severely damaged building was replaced in 1909 by an 84-foot, reinforced concrete tower with adjacent bay-style dwelling. The height of the octagonal tower allowed its light to be seen above the high walls of the military prison then under construction on the island.

For more than fifty years, the light station would share its rugged roost with prisons, both military and civilian. The infamous federal "pen" accepted its first prisoners in 1934. As a result, keepers here endured many sleepless days as well as nights during major breakouts and riots. The worst incident came in 1946 when inmates took over the prison, holding police and a contingent of U.S. Marines at bay for nearly two days. Both the lighthouse and its keeper survived

the uprising. The light was automated in 1963, not long before the doors of the prison slammed shut for the last time. Ironically, the two-story lighthouse keeper's residence, having survived both sea storms and prison riots, was badly burned during a protracted demonstration by young Native Americans in 1969.

TO SEE THE LIGHT: Alcatraz Island is part of the Golden Gate National Recreation Area; call (415) 705–5555. Tour boats leave for Alcatraz Island several times a day from Pier 41 in the Fisherman's Wharf district; call (415) 705–5555. A museum on the island displays the fourth-order Fresnel lens once used here; the station now employs a modern optic.

YERBA BUENA LIGHT

This light once guided dozens of passenger ferries passing back and forth each day between San Francisco and Oakland, and the U.S. Lighthouse Service once maintained a major depot on the island for storage of buoys, lenses, lamp oil, and other supplies and equipment. The Bay Bridge, opened in 1939, now carries most cross-bay traffic, but the light on Yerba Buena Island still shines. Nowadays, it mostly serves pleasure craft and the Coast Guard base, which takes up the entire 140-acre island. A Coast Guard admiral lives in the old keeper's dwelling, and the original fifth-order Fresnel lens still crowns the station's two-story octagonal tower and displays an occulting white light.

TO SEE THE LIGHT: Located on an active Coast Guard station, the lighthouse is not open to the public. Its light can be seen from the bay and from a variety of points along the shore. The lighthouse itself can be seen from the Bay Bridge, which links San Francisco to Oakland.

Location: San Francisco

Established: 1874

Tower height: 25 feet

Elevation of the focal plane: 95 feet

Optic: Modern

Status: Active

Characteristic: Occulting

Range: 14 miles

Position: 37° 48' 24
122° 21' 42

Note: Served as the West's largest lighthouse depot

U.S. Coast Guard

Location: Oakland

Launched: 1950

Status: Decommissioned and sold in 1975

Note: Served as a floating lighthouse

Lightship *WAL-605* rode at anchor for nearly ten years at Blunts Reef off Eureka. Launched in 1950 at a shipyard in East Boothbay, Maine, the *WAL-605*, as it was first called, was originally assigned to Overfalls Station near Cape May, New Jersey. In 1960 it was sent to the West for service at Blunts Reef, and during its last years on active duty served as a relief lightship at San Francisco Station or wherever it might be needed. The *WAL-605* has a steel hull 108 feet long with a 30-foot beam. The mushroom anchor, which so often held it firmly on station, weighs 7,000 pounds.

Sold as surplus property by the Coast Guard in 1975, the *WAL-605* functioned as a historical museum and even as a fishing boat. Today it is owned by the nonprofit U.S. Lighthouse Society, which is doing lighthouse lovers, students of maritime history, and the nation an enormous favor by restoring the old ship. (The Society also raises money for lighthouse restoration projects throughout America.)

TO SEE THE LIGHT: Open to the public on Saturday and Sunday, the lightship is berthed on the Oakland waterfront at Jack London Square. For more information call the U.S. Lighthouse Society at (510) 272-0544. The society can also provide a wealth of information on lighthouses and lightships throughout the United States and Canada, and on general lighthouse history. Write to U.S. Lighthouse Society, 244 Kearney Street, 5th Floor, San Francisco, CA 94108.

EAST BROTHER LIGHT

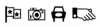

Built in 1874, the classically Victorian East Brother Lighthouse now serves as both a navigational light guiding vessels into San Pablo Bay, and as a popular bed-and-breakfast inn. Located on a small island just off San Pablo Point, the lighthouse marks the channel through the narrow and often treacherous San Pablo Straits that links the Sacramento River estuary to the open San Francisco Bay.

Unable to buy property on the mainland at an acceptable price, the government resorted to building the station on tiny East Brother Island. Construction crews had to blast away much of the one-third acre island in order to level the site. There was hardly room on what remained to squeeze the combination two-story tower and dwelling and separate fog signal building. In 1967 the Coast Guard decided to automate the station, place its light on a pole, and tear down the old buildings. Local preservationists managed to save the structure and, over time, restore the station to its original Victorian charm. The fifth-order light is still in operation.

TO SEE THE LIGHT: For overnight reservations at the East Brother Light Station call (510) 233–2385. Day visits are also encouraged. To the north, at 2000 Glenn Cove Drive in Vallejo, is the Carquinez Strait Lighthouse (1910), which once marked the western reaches of San Pablo Bay. Located off Route 780, this retired lighthouse is now privately owned, but visitors are welcome to walk the grounds.

Location: Richmond

Established: 1874

Tower height: 48 feet

Elevation of the focal plane: 61 feet

Optic: Modern

Status: Active

Characteristic: Flashes white every 5 seconds

Range: 17 miles

Position: 37° 57' 48
122° 61' 00

Note: Now an attractive offshore bed-and-breakfast

Nancy Pizzo

POINT BONITA LIGHT

uilt in 1855 on a high ledge more than 300 feet above the sea, the original station had a 56-foot brick tower and a detached, Cape Cod–style dwelling. Officials considered this lighthouse so important that they assigned it an exceptionally powerful second-order Fresnel lens. The light could be seen from up to 20 miles at sea, except in a heavy fog, which could make it completely invisible.

Since low-lying clouds frequently masked the beacon, the station needed an effective fog signal. Originally it was equipped only with a surplus army cannon that was fired off with an ear-splitting roar by the keepers whenever fog rolled in, which it did nearly every day. The cannon was eventually replaced by a 1,500-pound bell.

In time officials decided to build another lighthouse closer to the water, where its beacon would be more effective. Construction got under way in 1872, but fitting the new station onto the only available site—a frightfully narrow ledge about 120 feet above the waves—was no simple matter. To bring materials to the site, a landing platform, derrick, and incline railway had to be built, and a tunnel blasted through more than 100 feet of solid rock. It took more than five years to complete the 33-foot tower and associated structures. Equipped with the Fresnel lens from the original lighthouse and a pair of steam-driven fog sirens, the station was, at last, ready for service by the winter of 1877.

The lighthouse survived the earthquake that leveled much of San Francisco in 1906. During the 1940s, however, a landslide destroyed the land bridge that connected the tower and fog signal building. The Coast Guard first replaced it with a wooden bridge, then with the attractive suspension bridge that still serves the station today. In 1981 the Point Bonita Light became the last of California's lighthouses to be automated.

TO SEE THE LIGHT: This extraordinarily scenic lighthouse located off Highway 101 just north of San Francisco is now part of the Golden Gate National Recreation Area. From San Francisco cross the Golden Gate Bridge, take the Alexander Avenue exit, and follow Conzelman Road to the lighthouse. The winding roadway provides spectacular views of the city and the coast. You should bring sensible shoes since reaching the lighthouse requires a hike of more than 1 mile.

Location: San Francisco

Established: 1855

Tower height: 33 feet

Elevation of the focal plane: 124 feet

Optic: Modern

Status: Active

Characteristic: Occulting

Range: 18 miles

Position: 37° 48' 54
            122° 31' 48

Note: A scenic suspension bridge provides access

CHAPTER FOUR:
POINT REYES TO CRESCENT CITY

Marking the northern California coast may have been the greatest challenge ever undertaken by the U.S. Lighthouse Service. The sheer cliffs, rugged shores, and offshore rocks in this region required extreme exertions by craftsmen and laborers and costly outlays by an often reluctant Congress. As a result, progress was slow, but in time the work was completed because it had to be—lives depended on it.

Perhaps the most difficult task that faced lighthouse builders was construction of the light station on St. George Reef, a few miles west of Crescent City, California. In 1792 English explorer George Vancouver gave this deadly reef the name Dragon Rocks, and some commercial anglers still refer to it as "the Dragon." The name was later changed to St. George Reef, but whether medieval saint or dragon, the reef is a legend among mariners. Actually, this ship-killing obstacle is not a reef at all, but rather a submerged volcanic mountain. Its uppermost rocks reach just above the toss of the waves, out of sight to all but the sharpest-eyed sailor. The rocks rise abruptly from the sea, and there are no surrounding shallows to warn ships that they are approaching disaster. During rough weather breaking waves throw an obscuring blanket of mist over the rocks, making them practically invisible.

For the passengers and crew of the Civil War–era side-wheeler *Brother Jonathan*, the reef was a merciless sea monster. Plowing through heavy weather on the way to San Francisco, the *Brother Jonathan* slammed into the reef and sank in a matter of minutes. Nearly 200 lives were lost in the calamity. On land, the tragedy produced a scandal. Why had nothing been done to mark this obvious and death-dealing maritime hazard? The *Brother Jonathan* was not the only vessel to split open its hull on the reef's sharp rocks: A cemetery in Crescent City was filled with the graves of mariners who would have lived longer had it not been for St. George Reef.

Following the loss of the *Brother Jonathan*, the Lighthouse Board decided to take on the unprecedented challenge of building a lighthouse directly atop the exposed, wave-swept rocks of St. George Reef. To execute the daunting project, the board hired M.A. Ballantyne, who had built a lighthouse on Oregon's Tillamook Rock only the year before.

During winter 1882 Ballantyne and his men arrived off St.
George Reef in the 126-ton schooner *LaNinfa*. Weather conditions
were so rough that Ballantyne's surveyors and workers managed to
get onto the rocks only three times in a stretch of four weeks, but
by early spring work was under way. Ballantyne's formidable crew
of nearly fifty workers rigged a cable from the rocks' highest point—
about 54 feet—to the schooner, which had been secured with
heavy mooring tackle.

The sea was not the only problem faced by the builders. The
glycerin powder used for blasting out the foundation was highly
unstable, and an accidental explosion was always a threat. And
long stretches of generally horrible weather produced delays. So,
too, did lack of money. The original congressional appropriation had
been highly unrealistic, and soon bills began to stack up faster than
the stones of the light tower. Not until 1887 did Congress provide
sufficient funds for the structure to be completed. Eventually the
government spent a whopping $704,633 on the project, making
this the most expensive lighthouse in the nation's history.

The St. George Reef Lighthouse was at last placed in service
on October 20, 1892, more than ten years after construction got
under way. The station was considered too isolated and dangerous
for families, so most lighthouse personnel maintained homes on the
mainland. The station crew consisted of five men who worked four
weeks on and two weeks off. For obvious reasons, St. George
Lighthouse developed a reputation as one of the least popular and
most dangerous light stations in America. On several occasions
crewmen were killed while traveling to or from the reef. In 1951
three coastguardsmen were drowned in a single incident when
waves swamped the station launch.

In 1972 the Coast Guard abandoned the St. George Lighthouse
and replaced it with a buoy. The reef was then left unwatched and
untrammeled by humans, to carry on its ageless battle with the sea.

More recently, northern California lighthouse lovers have taken
charge of the venerable lighthouse and are restoring it one wall, iron
fitting, and window at a time. Their efforts are a fitting monument to
those who struggled to mark "the Dragon" and save the lives of
others. Indeed, all of California's lighthouses serve as similar monu-
ments, and each of them has much to teach us.

I n 1885, Point Reyes keeper E.G. Chamberlain wrote the following: "Solitude, where are your charms? . . . [B]etter dwell in the midst of alarms than in this horrible place." It is not hard to understand keeper Chamberlain's melancholy when one considers that Point Reyes is socked in by fog more than 110 days a year. Keepers lived and worked on this isolated and frequently shrouded point of land for more than a century and at times must have thought they were on another planet.

Considered one of the West's most dangerous navigational obstacles, Point Reyes sweeps more than 15 miles southwestward from the mostly southeastward-trending northern California coast. With its fog, wind, and tricky currents, the mostly low-lying point has been tearing open the hulls of ships since at least the sixteenth century.

Despite the number of ships run aground, centuries would pass before any determined effort was made to mark this prominent navigational hazard. Point Reyes was so rugged and remote that construction of a lighthouse here was thought impractical if not altogether impossible. After a rash of shipwrecks during and after the California gold rush, U.S. maritime officials decided that something had to be done, and in 1870 a lighthouse was finally built at the far seaward end of the point.

Fitted with a first-order Fresnel lens weighing more than two tons, the station warned mariners with an extraordinarily powerful light that could be seen for more than 24 miles. Shining out over the Pacific from an elevation of more than 280 feet, the beacon made navigation of this stretch of the California coast much safer.

Point Reyes was considered an unattractive duty station by most keepers, who found the fog and isolation hard to endure, but some apparently thrived on the seclusion. For instance, Gustav Zetterquist held the job of Point Reyes keeper from 1930 until 1951, a stretch of more than twenty years. The station was finally automated in 1975, much to the relief, no doubt, of some lonely keeper.

Although taken out of service in 1975, the station's huge Fresnel lens still dominates the sixteen-sided brick tower, which despite its lofty elevation is just shy of 40 feet tall. Maintained nowadays by park rangers at the Point Reyes National Seashore, the lens, with its sixteen separate bull's-eyes, fascinates visitors but no longer guides mariners. That task is handled by a modern optic mounted on top of the old fog signal building.

TO SEE THE LIGHT: The lighthouse is located in Point Reyes National Seashore off Route 1 northwest of San Francisco. Stop first at the Bear Valley visitor center near the entrance; call (415) 464–5100. An observation platform at the light station provides a fine view of the facility. A seemingly endless flight of 300 steps leads down to the tower; only visitors in good physical condition should attempt the climb. Keep in mind that the weather at Point Reyes is highly variable and unpredictable.

Location: Point Reyes National Seashore

Established: 1870

Tower height: 37 feet

Elevation of the focal plane: 285 feet

Optic: Modern

Status: Active

Characteristic: Flashes white every 5 seconds

Range: 20 miles

Position: 37° 59' 42 123° 01' 24

Note: Among the foggiest places in America

POINT ARENA LIGHT

Location: Point Arena

Established: 1870

Tower height: 115 feet

Elevation of the focal
plane: 155 feet

Optic: Modern

Status: Active

Characteristic: Flashes
white every 15 seconds

Range: 25 miles

Position: 38° 55' 17
            123° 44' 26

Note: America's first
reinforced concrete
lighthouse

L ike much of the California coastline, Point Arena turns a
hospitable face to those who come by land, but bares its teeth
to mariners. Jagged, saw-toothed rocks rise from the waves just
offshore and 2.5 miles to the west, predatory Point Arena Rock rises
from the sea, waiting to tear open the hulls of ships. Since 1870 the
powerful, flashing beacon of the Point Arena Lighthouse has warned
vessels of these dangers.

The original station consisted not only of a tower, dwelling, and
outbuildings, but also had a pair of 12-inch steam whistles protruding
from the roof of a specially built fog-signal building. The steam for the
whistles was generated by wood-burning boilers that consumed up
to 100 tons of firewood during especially foggy years. Keepers not
only had to tend the light and feed the hungry boilers, but also brace
themselves against the constant threat of storms and earthquakes.

The point's rugged topography was created by movement of
the San Andreas Fault, which lies beneath the lighthouse. The
legendary fault slipped and growled in 1906, flattening much of San
Francisco and, not surprisingly, devastating the Point Arena light
station. Fatally cracked by the earthquake, the original brick tower
could not be repaired and had to be torn down and replaced. To
buttress the new, 115-foot tower against future quakes, builders
reinforced its concrete walls with steel. The first-order Fresnel lens
placed here in 1908 remains in the tower, but nowadays the station's
powerful flashing beacon is produced by an efficient modern optic
located outside the lantern room.

TO SEE THE LIGHT: Located about 1 mile north of Point Arena off
Lighthouse Road, the lighthouse is open to the public daily. For more
information call Point Arena Lighthouse at (877) 725–4448. A
museum in the old fog signal building recounts the station's history.

POINT CABRILLO LIGHT

The sea and land have never been good neighbors at Point Cabrillo. Storm-driven waves often slam against the shore, hurling salt spray onto rocks near the top of 60-foot cliffs. Fog rises off the ocean to blanket the point for as much as 1,000 hours each year. Weather makes this coast perilous for mariners and dreary for lighthouse personnel, but for nearly sixty-five years keepers and their assistants have lived and worked here full time.

Since 1909 a small clapboard fog signal building and attached octagonal wooden light tower have guarded this lonely headland and warned mariners to steer clear. The building looks more like a country church or school than a lighthouse, and that seems fitting, for keepers and their families have lived a bucolic existence at Point Cabrillo. In addition to maintaining the light, keepers often raised vegetables and looked after cows, pigs, and chickens. This decidedly rural life came to an end in 1973 when the station was automated and the last of the keepers packed up and headed for town or other Coast Guard assignments.

During the years after automation, the station's third-order Fresnel lens gave way to a more easily maintained airport-style beacon. No longer needed, the tower, fog signal building, and other structures fell into disrepair and, in time, might have been demolished had not lighthouse preservationists stepped in to save them. Currently the station is undergoing a full-scale restoration funded by the California Coastal Conservancy and the North Coast Interpretive Association, a local nonprofit group. As part of the restoration, the station's original third-order Fresnel lens has been repaired and put back into the tower where it once more serves mariners.

It is fortunate that anything remained of the lighthouse to be restored. Time and demolition crews were not the station's only enemies. On more than one occasion the Pacific Ocean itself has threatened to carry away the lighthouse. In 1960 a gale struck Point Cabrillo with such force that two-ton boulders were thrown up onto the cliffs by waves that rolled over the fields and into the heavy doors on the seaward side of the tower.

Location: Mendocino

Established: 1909

Tower height: 47 feet

Elevation of the focal plane: 81 feet

Optic: Fresnel lens (third order)

Status: Active

Characteristic: Flashes white every 10 seconds

Range: 22 miles

Position: 39° 20' 54
              123° 49' 36

Note: Restored Fresnel lens once more guides mariners

TO SEE THE LIGHT: Public access to the tower and other structures is limited during restoration, but visitors are welcome to walk
the grounds. A few miles north of Mendocino or approximately 6
miles south of Fort Bragg, turn off Highway 1 onto Point Cabrillo
Road. Take Lighthouse Road to the station. For more information call
the North Coast Interpretive Association at (707) 937–0816.

PUNTA GORDA LIGHTHOUSE

A rounded, nearly treeless cape thrusting 800 feet above the sea, Punta Gorda rises above the northern California coast like a fist waiting to smash vessels that venture too close to its jagged rocks. Eight ships were lost near Punta Gorda between 1899 and 1907. The last of these, the *Columbia*, took eighty-seven people down with her. Prompted by these disasters, Congress funded a light station in 1908, but building the new lighthouse was not easy. Materials had to be landed well to the north of the site and then dragged down the beach on horse-drawn sleds. Nonetheless, by 1912, the tower's fourth-order Fresnel lens began to cast its flashing light toward the sea.

Since it was as difficult to maintain as it had been to build, the lighthouse was abandoned by the Coast Guard as soon as it became practical to do so. The station was closed permanently in 1951, and the lighthouse fell into ruin. Most station buildings were burned in the 1970s to keep out squatters. All that remains today is a single-story concrete watch room with a spiral staircase leading to an iron lantern room overhead. Resting on a bluff 48 feet above the surf, the entire structure stands only 27 feet high.

TO SEE THE LIGHT: From U.S. Highway 101 in northern California, take the Cape Mendocino Road from Fortuna and follow it to the village of Petrolia. A 3.5-mile trail leads to the lighthouse.

Location: Petrolia

Established: 1912

Status: Deactivated in 1951

Note: Only the gutted tower still stands

U.S. Coast Guard

CAPE MENDOCINO LIGHTHOUSE

California's westernmost point is also one of its most imposing headlands. Cape Mendocino's soaring 1,400-foot cliffs drop almost vertically into the Pacific. Although the cape was among the West's best known seamarks and most feared navigational obstacles, no light was placed here until the late 1860s.

Establishing a lighthouse on the cape proved a daunting challenge. The first ship bringing supplies to the construction site wrecked on the merciless rocks to the south. When a second ship finally delivered the necessary materials, they had to be hoisted with ropes hundreds of feet up the cliffs. Laborers were forced to endure weeks of rain and fog and to camp out in howling winds. Despite the difficulties, workers eventually completed a two-story brick dwelling and barn and erected a sixteen-sided iron tower that had been prefabricated by machinists in San Francisco.

Focused by a first-order Fresnel lens, its beacon first lit the cape on the night of December 1, 1868. With a focal plane more than 400 feet above the Pacific, the light could be seen from more than 25 miles at sea. Deactivated during the 1970s (a light still marks the cape, but it shines from a pole located on the cliffs about 500 feet above the Pacific; it displays a flashing white light with a range of 19 miles), the old lighthouse stood empty for decades. In 1998 the nearly ruined metal tower was moved to Shelter Cove, where it now graces a small park.

Location: Capetown

Established: 1868

Tower height: 43 feet

Status: Deactivated in 1975

Note: Tower removed and put on display in Shelter Cove

TO SEE THE LIGHT: Near Garberville on U.S. Highway 101, take the Redway exit, drive west following the signs to Shelter Cove. The Cape Mendocino tower is in Mal Coombs Park off Machi Road.

HUMBOLDT HARBOR LIGHTHOUSE

C ompleted in 1856, at a time when much of the U.S. Pacific coast was still a wilderness, the Humboldt Harbor Lighthouse was among the first light stations in the West. Built at a cost of $15,000, it consisted of a Cape Cod–style dwelling with a 21-foot tower rising through the middle section of its roof. The lantern room held a fourth-order Fresnel lens.

Built on a sandy foundation, the lighthouse was threatened by nature almost from the beginning. Wracked by earthquakes, storms, and beach erosion, the structure began to deteriorate. In 1885 a cyclone tore away its roof and drove floating logs against its walls. The building was repaired, but soon its masonry began to crack and fall apart. In the 1930s it eventually collapsed into a jumble of masonry on the beach.

TO SEE THE LIGHT: Nothing remains of this historic station except for a few chunks of masonry occasionally washed up on Humboldt Bay beaches.

Location: Eureka

Established: 1856

Status: Abandoned in 1892 and destroyed in the 1930s

Note: One of California's earliest lighthouses

TABLE BLUFF LIGHTHOUSE

A fter the Humboldt Harbor Lighthouse was severely damaged by a gale, it was replaced by a new lighthouse (pictured) built high atop nearby Table Bluff. A Victorian-style structure with an attached, square tower, it was given the same fourth-order lens that had once shone from the tower of the harbor lighthouse. Although the Table Bluff tower was only 35 feet tall, its elevation placed the light approximately 190 feet above the bay. The light could be seen from up to 20 miles away.

After more than eighty years of service, the Table Bluff Lighthouse was decommissioned in 1972 and turned over to a private foundation. The tower of the lighthouse was cut into two parts and trucked to Woodley Island near Eureka, where it was reassembled, repaired, and refitted with the station's old Fresnel lens. Today it serves as a tourist attraction and a reminder of the area's rich maritime history.

During nearly a century of service, the Table Bluff Lighthouse marked the entrance to Humbolt Bay, which provided access to Eureka, so named perhaps because the locals hoped to find gold in mountains behind the town. Instead, they made fortunes on the region's redwood forests, converting them to lumber for shipment to San Francisco and other important western ports.

TO SEE THE LIGHT: The Table Bluff tower stands on Woodley Island in the Eureka Inner Harbor area. Follow U.S. Highway 101 into Eureka, turn toward the water on Route 255, and follow signs to the lighthouse. The nearby Humboldt Bay Maritime Museum has the station's fourth-order Fresnel lens on display; call (707) 444–9440.

Location: Eureka

Established: 1892

Tower height: 35 feet

Elevation of the focal plane: 190 feet

Optic: Fresnel lens (fourth order)

Status: Deactivated in 1972

Note: Tower on display at marina

Bob and Sandra Shanklin, The Lighthouse People

TRINIDAD HEAD LIGHT

Set on a jagged cliff face almost 200 feet above the Pacific, this little lighthouse has aided commercial anglers and other mariners seeking the shelter of Trinidad Harbor for more than a century. Built in 1871 to guide schooners carrying lumber to San Francisco, the light helped close a gap of darkness between Crescent City and Humboldt Bay to the south. While the station's fourth-order Fresnel lens was small for a coastal light, the elevation of the tower, which was perched on a high cliff, made its beacon visible from up to 20 miles at sea. When the light was automated in 1947, its classical lens was replaced by an airport-style beacon.

TO SEE THE LIGHT: Take the Trinidad exit from U.S. Highway 101 and drive toward the harbor. The Trinidad Head Lighthouse is closed to the public, but hiking trails lead to an overlook with a view of the old lighthouse. Less energetic visitors have another attractive option: a replica of the tower has been built in town. It is a near-perfect match of the original and now houses the antique Fresnel lens that served for so many years at the Trinidad Head station.

Location: Trinidad
Established: 1871
Tower height: 25 feet
Elevation of the focal plane: 196 feet
Optic: Modern
Status: Active
Characteristic: Occulting
Range: 14 miles
Position: 41° 03' 06
124° 09' 06

The light tower shown here is only a memorial. The real—and still active—Trinidad Head Light stands on the seaward side of the mountain in the background.
Nancy Pizzo

BATTERY POINT LIGHT

P ressed by northern California lumber interests, Congress designated Crescent City as a site for one of the West's earliest lighthouses. Like many other western light stations, this one consisted of a simple Cape Cod–style dwelling with a tower rising through the center of its roof. Beginning in 1856 the beacon, focused by its fourth-order Fresnel lens, guided freighters into the city's bustling harbor, then out again bearing loads of redwood bound for San Francisco.

Captain John Jeffrey and his wife, Nellie, took over keeper's duties at the Crescent City Lighthouse in 1875. They became near-permanent fixtures of the station. In all, they spent thirty-nine years in the lighthouse and raised four children there.

The thick stone walls of the lighthouse, built for a mere $15,000, outlasted several generations of keepers. They still stand today, little changed from the station's earliest days. Except for a stroke of luck, however, the station's last night might have been that of March 27, 1964. The earthquake that hit Alaska on that date sent five titanic tidal waves hurtling toward the coast of northern California, where they stormed ashore shortly after midnight. Keepers Clarence and Peggy Coons saw them coming but could do little about the situation. Fortunately, the enormous waves struck at such an extreme angle that the lighthouse and its keepers were spared.

Although discontinued in 1965, the light was reestablished in 1982 as a private aid to navigation. The building now serves as both a history museum and active lighthouse with resident keepers.

TO SEE THE LIGHT: The lighthouse and museum are located at Battery Point on the west side of Crescent City Harbor. Write to Del Norte County Historical Society, P.O. Box 396, Crescent City, CA 95531 or call (707) 464–3922.

Location: Crescent City

Established: 1856

Tower height: 37 feet

Elevation of the focal plane: 285 feet

Optic: Fresnel lens (fourth order)

Status: Private aid to navigation

Characteristic: Flashes white every 30 seconds

Range: 14 miles

Position: 41° 44' 36
            124° 12' 06

Note: Operating light-house and museum with resident keepers

ST. GEORGE REEF LIGHT

B uilt on an exposed rock constantly pounded by the Pacific, the St. George Reef Light cost the U.S. government $704,633, making it the most expensive lighthouse in the nation's history. Mariners who long dreaded this deadly obstacle certainly thought the money well spent. Over the centuries this notorious reef had ruined numerous ships including the side-wheeler *Brother Jonathan*, wrecked here in 1865 with a loss of more than 200 lives.

The hulking and costly stone tower was erected on a giant elliptical base of granite and concrete. Rising more than 140 feet above the waves, the tower originally held a first-order Fresnel lens displaying an alternating red and white flashing light.

After the U.S. Coast Guard discontinued this light in 1975, local lighthouse lovers wondered what would become of this legendary station. During the late 1990s they resolved to restore the historic station and to that purpose formed the St. George Reef Lighthouse Preservation Society. The effort suffered a setback in 2002 when the station's original lantern was accidentally destroyed while being moved ashore for restoration. Undeterred, the society had an exact replica built and placed atop the tower. Later that year the station's light was relit, and it now serves as a private aid to navigation.

TO SEE THE LIGHT: This spectacular light station and its restored beacon can be seen from the end of Crescent City's Washington Boulevard. The station's 18-foot-high, first-order Fresnel lens is on display in the Del Norte County Historical Society museum on Sixth Street in Crescent City; call (707) 464–3922. Helicopter tours are offered on a limited basis; call the St. George Reef Lighthouse Preservation Society at (707) 464–8299.

Location: Crescent City

Established: 1892

Tower height: 90 feet

Elevation of the focal plane: 144 feet

Optic: Fresnel lens (fourth order)

Status: Private aid to navigation

Characteristic: Flashes white every 12 seconds

Range: 20 miles

Position: 41° 50' 14
124° 23' 11

Note: Restored and returned to operation in 2002

GLOSSARY

Automated light

A lighthouse with no keeper. Following World War II, remote-control systems, light-activated switches, and fog-sensing devices made automation an increasingly cost-effective and attractive option, and the efficiency-minded Coast Guard automated one light station after another. By 1970 only about sixty lighthouses had full-time keepers, and within two decades all but one of those beacons had been automated. All of California's active lighthouses are now automated.

Beacon

A light or radio signal intended to guide mariners or aviators.

Breakwater light

Often harbors are protected from high waves by a lengthy barrier of stone called a breakwater. Because they rise only a few feet above the surface, breakwaters are hard to see, especially at night, and may threaten vessels entering or exiting the harbor. Breakwater beacons are meant to make mariners aware of this hazard and allow them to safely navigate the harbor entrance. For obvious reasons the light tower usually is placed near the end of the breakwater.

Cast-iron towers

Introduced as a building material during the 1840s, cast iron revolutionized lighthouse construction. Stronger than stone and relatively light, cast iron made it possible to fabricate parts of a light tower in a far-off foundry and then ship them to the construction site for assembly. A cylindrical structure assembled in 1844 on Long Island Head in Boston Harbor may have been the first all-cast-iron lighthouse.

Characteristic

The identifying feature of a lighthouse beacon. To help mariners distinguish one beacon from another, maritime officials give each light in a given region a distinct color or pattern of flashes. Among the more famous lighthouse characteristics is that of the offshore Minot's Ledge Lighthouse near Scituate, Massachusetts, which displays a single flash, followed by four quick flashes, then three more. This one-four-three flashing sequence reminds some romantic observers of I-LOVE-YOU.

Coast Guard, U.S.

Since 1939 lighthouses and other aids to navigation in the United States have been the responsibility of the U.S. Coast Guard. Previously, the nation's maritime lights were maintained by a separate government agency known as the U.S. Lighthouse Service.

Elevation or height of the focal plane

Fresnel lenses and most modern optical systems channel light signals into a narrow band known as the focal plane. Since the curvature of the earth would render low-lying lights practically worthless for navigation, a coastal beacon must have an elevated focal plane. The height of the plane above the water's surface—usually from 40 to 200 feet—helps determine the distance or range from which the light can be seen.

Fixed signal

A lighthouse beacon that shines constantly during its regular hours of operation is said to display a "fixed" signal.

Flashing signal

A lighthouse beacon that turns on and off or grows much brighter at regular intervals is called a flashing signal.

Focal plane

See Elevation or height of the focal plane

Fog signal or foghorn

A distinct sound signal, usually a horn, trumpet, or siren, used to warn vessels away from prominent headlands or navigational obstacles during fog or other periods of low visibility.

Fresnel lenses

Invented in 1822 by Augustin Fresnel, a noted French physicist, Fresnel lenses concentrate light into a powerful beam that can be seen over great distances. Usually they consist of individual hand-polished glass prisms arrayed in a bronze frame. Manufactured by a number of French and British companies, these devices came in as many as eleven different sizes or "orders." A massive first-order lens may be more than 6 feet in diameter and 12 feet tall, while a diminutive sixth-order lens is only about 1 foot wide and not much larger than an ordinary gallon jug.

Gallery

A circular walkway with a railing around the lantern of a lighthouse. Galleries provided keepers convenient access to the outside of the lantern for window cleaning, painting, and repair work.

Harbor light

A beacon intended to assist vessels moving in and out of a harbor. Not meant to serve as major coastal markers, harbor lights often consisted of little more than a lantern hung from a pole. However, many were official light stations with a tower and residence for the keeper.

Keeper

Before the era of automation, responsibility for operating and main-taining a light station was placed in the hands of a keeper, some-times aided by one or more assistants. During the eighteenth and nineteenth centuries, keepers were appointed by the Treasury Department or even the president himself in return for military service or a political favor. Although the work was hard and the pay minimal, these appointments were coveted since they offered a steady income, free housing, and no specific background or training was required.

Keeper's residence or dwelling

The presence of a keeper's residence is what turned a light station into a light "house." Sometime keepers lived in the tower itself, but a typical lighthouse dwelling was a detached one-and-a-half-story wood or stone structure built in a style similar to that of other working-class homes in the area.

Lamp and reflector

For several decades prior to the introduction of the highly efficient Fresnel lens, lighthouse beacons were intensified by means of lamp-and-reflector systems. These combined a bright-burning lamp and a polished mirror shaped in a manner intended to concentrate the light.

Lantern

The glass-enclosed space at the top of a light tower. It houses the lens (or optic) and protects it from the weather.

Light station

A navigational facility with a light beacon. Often the term is used interchangeably with "lighthouse," but a light station may not include a tower, quarters for a keeper, or a fog signal.

Light tower

A tall, often cylindrical, structure used to elevate a navigational light so that mariners can see it from a distance. Modern light towers support a lantern, which houses a lamp, electric beacon, or some other lighting device. Some light towers are an integral part of the keeper's residence, but most are detached.

Lighthouse

A term applied to a wide variety of buildings constructed for the purpose of guiding ships. Often it is used interchangeably with similar or derivative terms such as "light tower," "light station," or simply "light."

Lighthouse Board

Beginning in 1851 and for more than half a century afterward, U.S. lighthouses were administered by the nine-member Lighthouse Board. Usually board members were noted engineers, scientists, or military men. Creation of the Board brought a fresh professional spirit and penchant for innovation to the Lighthouse Service. Perhaps the Board's most significant contribution was its adoption of the advanced Fresnel lens as the standard U.S. lighthouse optic.

Lighthouse Service

A common term applied to the various organizations or agencies that built and maintained U.S. lighthouses from 1789 until 1939, when the Coast Guard was placed in charge.

Lightships

Equipped with their own beacons, usually displayed from a tall central mast, lightships were essentially floating lighthouses. They marked shoals or key navigational turning points where construction of a permanent light tower was either impossible or prohibitively expensive.

Modern optic

A term referring to a broad array of lightweight, mostly weather-proof devices that produce the most modern navigational lights.

Occulting or eclipsing light

There are several ways to produce a beacon that appears to flash. One is to "occult" or block the light at regular intervals, often with a rotating opaque panel.

Private aid to navigation

A privately owned and maintained navigational light. Often, such lights are formerly deactivated beacons that have been reestablished for historic or aesthetic purposes.

Skeleton towers

Iron or steel skeleton light towers consisting of four or more heavily braced metal legs topped by workrooms and/or a lantern. Relatively durable and inexpensive, they were built in considerable numbers during the latter half of the nineteenth century. Since their open walls offer little resistance to wind and water, these towers proved ideal for offshore navigational stations, but some, such as the sturdy skeleton tower on Point Loma near San Diego, were built on land.

Solar-powered optic

Nowadays, many remote lighthouse beacons are powered by batteries recharged during the day by solar panels.

Wickies

Before electric power made lighthouse work much cleaner and simpler, nearly all navigational beacons were produced by oil or kerosene lamps. Most of these lamps had wicks that required constant care and trimming. Consequently, lighthouse keepers often referred to themselves somewhat humorously as "wickies."

The still-functioning East Brother Light offers travelers a unique bed-and-breakfast experience.

ABOUT THE AUTHORS

Photographs by **Bruce Roberts** have appeared in numerous magazines, including *Life* and *Sports Illustrated*, and in hundreds of books, many of them about lighthouses. He was director of photography at *Southern Living* magazine for many years. His work is also on display in the permanent collection at the Smithsonian Institution. He lives in Morehead City, North Carolina.

Ray Jones is the author or coauthor of fourteen best-selling books about lighthouses. He has served as an editor at Time-Life Books, as founding editor of *Albuquerque Living* magazine, as writing coach at *Southern Living* magazine, and as founding publisher of Country Roads Press. He lives in Pebble Beach, California, where he continues to write about lighthouses and serves as a consultant to businesses, publishers, and other authors.

ALSO BY BRUCE ROBERTS AND RAY JONES

Lighthouses of Florida
A Guidebook and Keepsake

Lighthouses of Massachusetts
A Guidebook and Keepsake

Lighthouses of Michigan
A Guidebook and Keepsake

New England Lighthouses
Maine to Long Island Sound

American Lighthouses
A Comprehensive Guide

Eastern Great Lakes Ligthouses
Ontario, Erie, and Huron

Western Great Lakes Lighthouses
Michigan and Superior

Gulf Coast Lighthouses
Florida Keys to the Rio Grande

Mid-Atlantic Coast Lighthouses
Hudson River to Chesapeake Bay

Pacific Northwest Lighthouses
Oregon, Washington, Alaska, and British Columbia

Southern Lighthouses
Outer Banks to Cape Florida